OXFORD

UNIVERSITY PRESS

Hot and Cold

Lesley Pether

A fire is hot. It makes things hot.

Fire makes us hot.

3

Snow is cold. It makes things cold.

4

Snow makes everything cold.

The sun is hot.

It makes us hot.

7

Ice is cold.

It makes everything **cold**.

A cooker is hot.

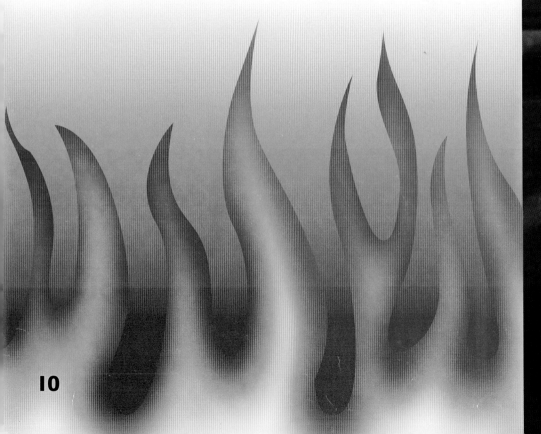

A cooker makes food hot.

A freezer is cold. It makes food cold.

We put food in the freezer to make it **cold**.

Lava is hot.

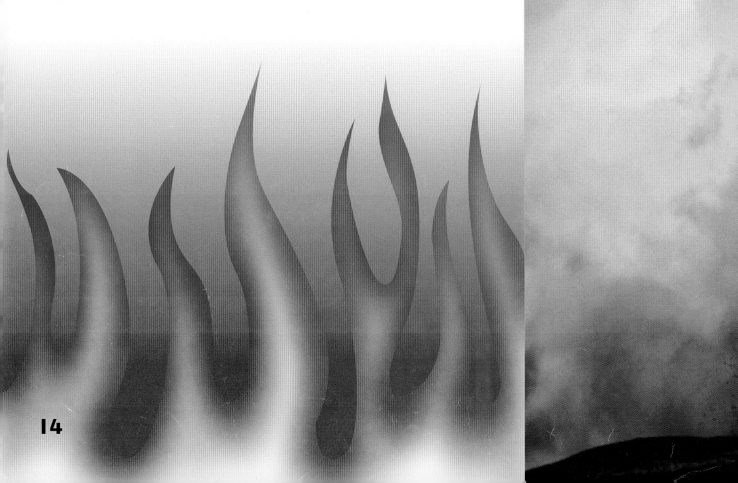

Lava is very hot!

15

Hot and Cold

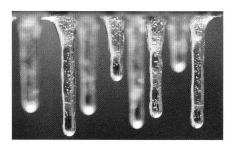

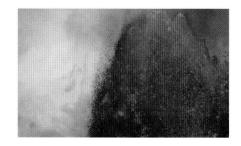